REMEMBER
YOU ARE A
FUCKING
GODDESS

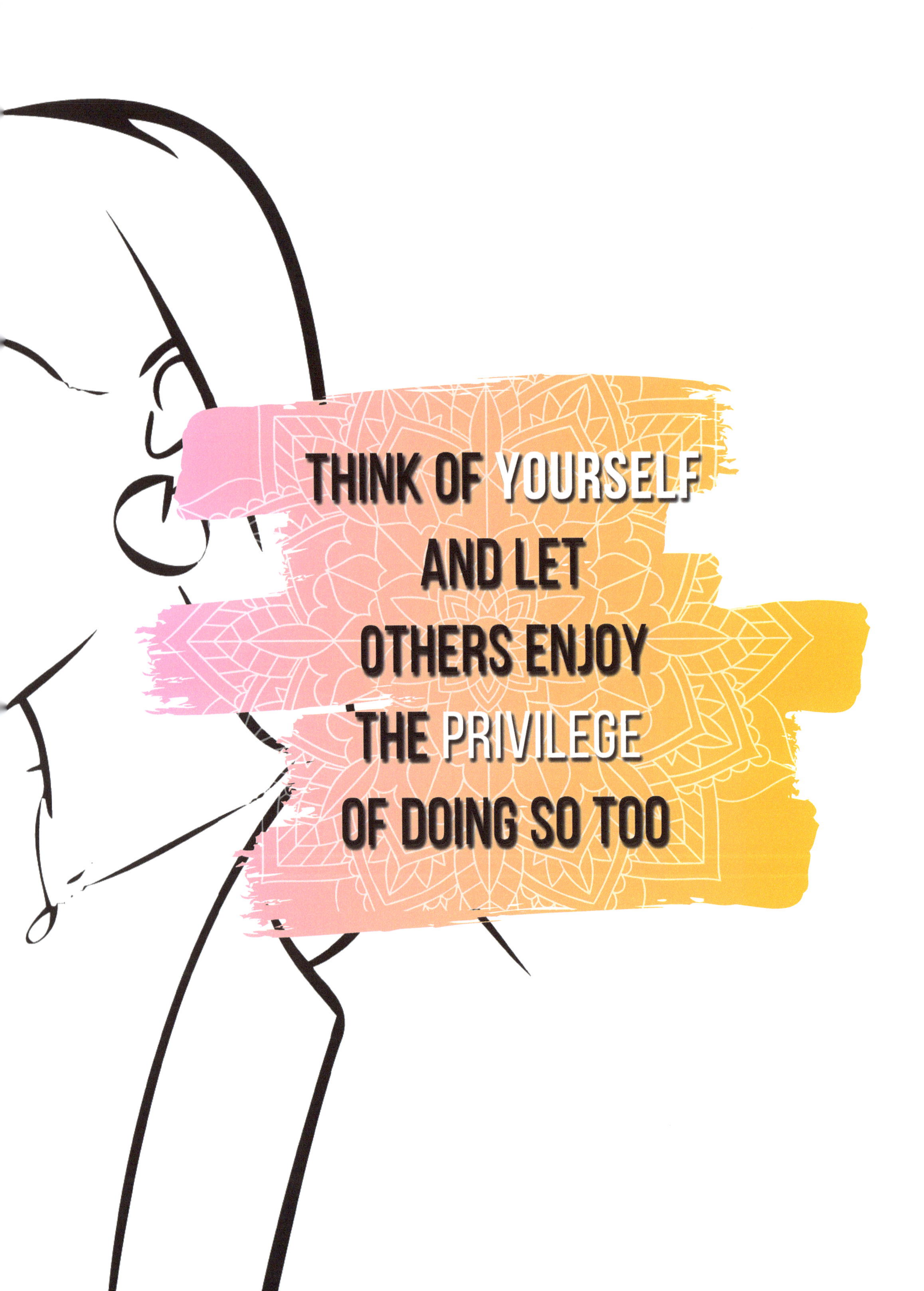

THINK OF YOURSELF
AND LET
OTHERS ENJOY
THE PRIVILEGE
OF DOING SO TOO

IF SOMEONE
TELLS YOU THAT
YOU LOOK FAMILIAR
TELL THEM
"I DO PORN"

STOP FIGHTING
YOUR INNER DEMONS
THINGS GO MUCH
SMOOTHER
WHEN YOU'RE ON
THE SAME SIDE

SMILE AT PEOPLE
WHO DON'T LIKE YOU
IT'LL REALLY
FREAK THEM OUT

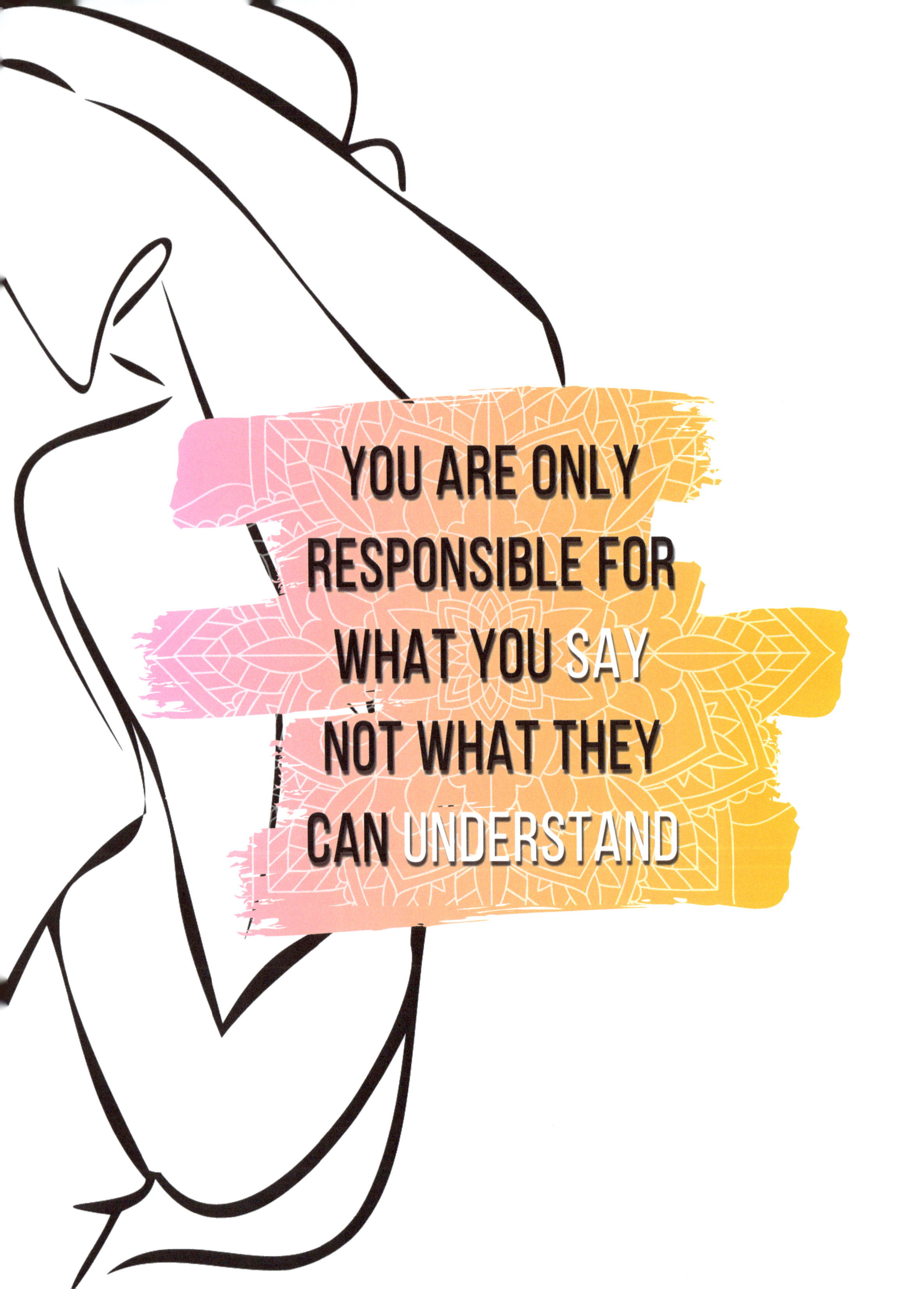
YOU ARE ONLY
RESPONSIBLE FOR
WHAT YOU SAY
NOT WHAT THEY
CAN UNDERSTAND

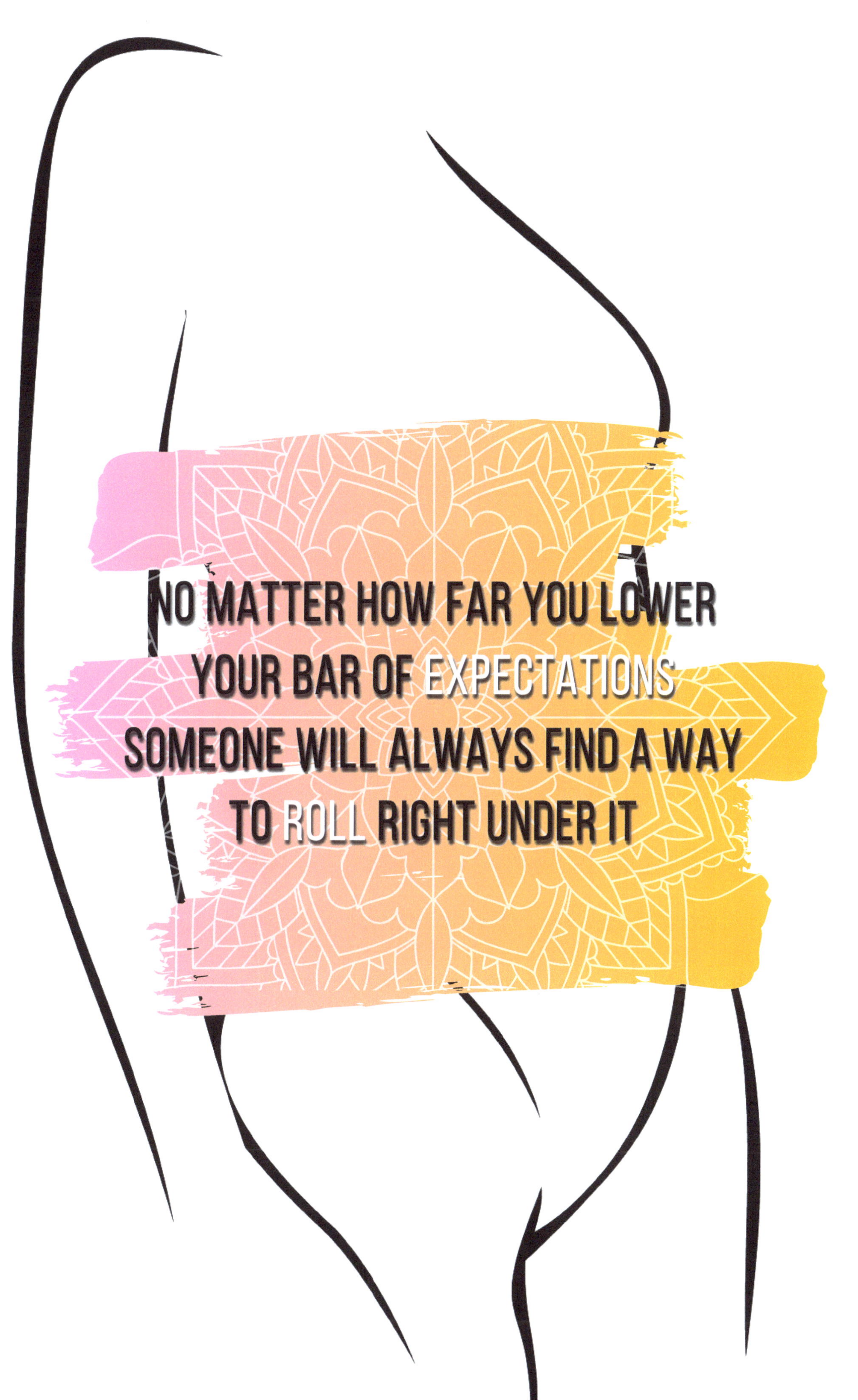
NO MATTER HOW FAR YOU LOWER
YOUR BAR OF EXPECTATIONS
SOMEONE WILL ALWAYS FIND A WAY
TO ROLL RIGHT UNDER IT

YOU'VE GOT THIS
REMEMBER
YOU'RE AN
UNSTOPPABLE
BADASS

DON'T BE ASHAMED
OF WHO YOU ARE
THAT'S YOUR PARENTS JOB

DON'T GO CRAZY
BE CRAZY
JUST GO NORMAL
FROM TIME TO TIME

DON'T GIVE UP
JUST SCREAM
FUCK
AS LOUD AS YOU CAN
AND KEEP CLIMBING

TAKE A DEEP BREATH
AND REMEMBER
WHO THE FUCK YOU ARE

DON'T JUST SPEW
YOUR CUSS WORDS
ENUNCIATE THEM CLEARLY.
REMEMBER,
YOU'RE A FUCKING LADY

YOU CAN'T DO
EPIC SHIT
WITH BASIC PEOPLE

FUCK PERFECT.
EMBRACE YOUR FLAWS
BE DIFFERENT
BE WILD
LOVE EVERY MOMENT OF IT

YOU FUCKING CAN
AND
YOU FUCKING WILL

HOLY
FUCK
YOU ARE
FUCKING SEXY

EITHER FIND A WAY
OR FUCKING
MAKE YOUR OWN

IF YOU OWN
YOUR STORY
MAKE SURE IT HAS
A FUCKING EPIC
ENDING

STOP OVERTHINKING
EVERYTHING
IF IT FUCKING
MAKES YOU HAPPY
DO IT

YOUR INTUITION
TENDS TO KNOW HER SHIT

KEEP PUSHING
REMEMBER
YOU HAVE A LOT OF
MOTHERFUCKERS
TO PROVE WRONG

GUESS WHAT.
A REAL WOMAN
IS WHATEVER
THE ABSOLUTE FUCK
SHE WANTS TO BE.

JUST BECAUSE THEY'RE
COLORBLIND
DOESN'T MEAN YOU AREN'T
A RAINBOW

BE GLAD THEY
WENT AND FUCKED UP
THEY DIDN'T
DESERVE YOU ANYWAY